Dad took Kipper to school.

1

They went past the library.

A lady was painting the wall.

Kipper ran into the playground.

He wanted to play.

There was a drawing on the wall.

It was a drawing of Kipper.

The wall looked a mess.

Mrs May was cross.

The children were painting.

Kipper had an idea.

Miss Green drew circles on the wall.

The children painted faces.

The wall looked good.

Everyone liked it.

'Good for Kipper!' everyone said.